symFUNNY

Jeannie Fleming-Gifford & Anna J. Magnusson
Illustrated by Kira Weber

"Music gives soul to the universe, wings to the mind, flight to the
imagination, and charm and gaiety
to life and to everything." - Plato

This book is dedicated to those who love, inspire, celebrate
and educate children about the joy of music.
Thank you to our families who supported and encouraged
us to share our gifts and passion for writing,
art and music with the community.

ISBN: 978-1-7333668-9-2

Printed in the United States of America

Editing by Joanne Fenton Humphrey

Windjammer Adventure Publishing
289 South Franklin Street, Chagrin Falls, OH 44022
Telephone 440.247.6610   Email windjammerpub@mac.com

The story *behind* the story.

Many years ago, Jeannie Fleming-Gifford and Anna J. Magnusson connected in Columbus, OH, both having a mutual love for the arts and writing. Together, the two began creating and collaborating on a variety of stories.

SymFUNNY was inspired by watching young children enter the orchestra hall, many for the first time, to experience a live performance of the Columbus Symphony Orchestra where Fleming-Gifford worked as the education director for several years. The concept came to life as Anna and Jeannie captured the viewpoint of young children and their expectations of going to the symphony versus their actual experience.

The manuscript sat waiting to be shared until Fleming-Gifford connected with Kira Weber, a Chagrin Falls based artist who shared her time and talents at Fairmount Center for the Arts where Fleming-Gifford is the executive director. Weber's artistic talents were quickly noticed and after attending an art opening of Weber's, Jeannie contacted Anna with an "a-ha" moment...Kira was the perfect fit for bringing the concept of *SymFUNNY* to print.

Whether this playful children's story is shared as an introduction to symphonic music, the orchestra, to support literacy development or to simply connect with a young child in your life through time spent reading, we hope you will enjoy your time together with *SymFUNNY.*

About the Authors & Illustrator:

Jeannie Fleming-Gifford has a master's degree in child development and is the executive director at Fairmount Center for the Arts, a non-profit organization whose mission is to enrich lives through the arts. Her passions include outdoor adventures, volunteering to raise potential autism service dogs and writing.

Anna J. Magnusson serves as the executive director of the Iowa Able Foundation, a non-profit organization dedicated to empowering individuals with disabilities to achieve and maintain independence. She also volunteers as the producer and host of the *I Am Able IOWA* radio show that discusses the ability in disability.

Kira Weber is an artist in Chagrin Falls, Ohio. Her interest in art was evident before she could talk. As soon as she could hold a crayon, she began creating intricately detailed art. Her autism has helped her focus for extended periods as she paints and draws. *SymFUNNY* is Kira's first book project.

Proceeds from this book will support:

Fairmount Center for the Arts, a non-profit arts organization whose mission is to enrich lives through the arts. www.fairmountcenter.org

I Am Able IOWA is a radio program produced by the non-profit organization, AbleUp IOWA. The radio show discusses the ability in disability by sharing information, events, and stories with listeners. www.iamableiowa.com

"We're going to the symphony!" Mama exclaimed.

"The symFUNNY?" Alex asked.

"Yes," said Mama. "We will enjoy a wonderful time!"

"What will be at the symfunny?" Alex continued.

"You will see and hear many new and amazing things," Mama promised.

"I want to know more about the symfunny!" Alex said.

Symphony/Symfunny* (*Symfunny is just a silly word!)

"Of course, there will be notes floating in the air," Mama explained.
Alex imagined what she would see...

Notes/Notes

"...and cords"

Cords/Chords

"...and scales"

Scales/Scales

"There will be horns..."
Alex imagined the horns she would see...

honk honk

Horns/Horns

"...and lots of strings"

Strings/Strings

"Of course, there will be notes floating in the air," Mama explained.
Alex imagined what she would see...

Notes/Notes

"I am so excited! I can't wait to go the symfunny!
It sounds like a silly place!"

And so Mama and Alex went to the symphony.

But...

Symphony (not SymFUNNY, that's just a silly word!)

There were not any horns.
There were horns.

Horns/Horns

There was not a base, but there was a bass.

Base/Bass

There were not any strings, but there were many strings.

Strings/Strings

There was not a conductor who led a train, but there was a conductor who led beautiful music.

Conductor / Conductor

And the notes, chords, and scales were not seen, but Alex and Mama heard them.

Chords/Cords
Notes/Notes
Scales/Scales

And as the music ended, Alex declared that the symphony was NOT funny at all.

It was beautiful!

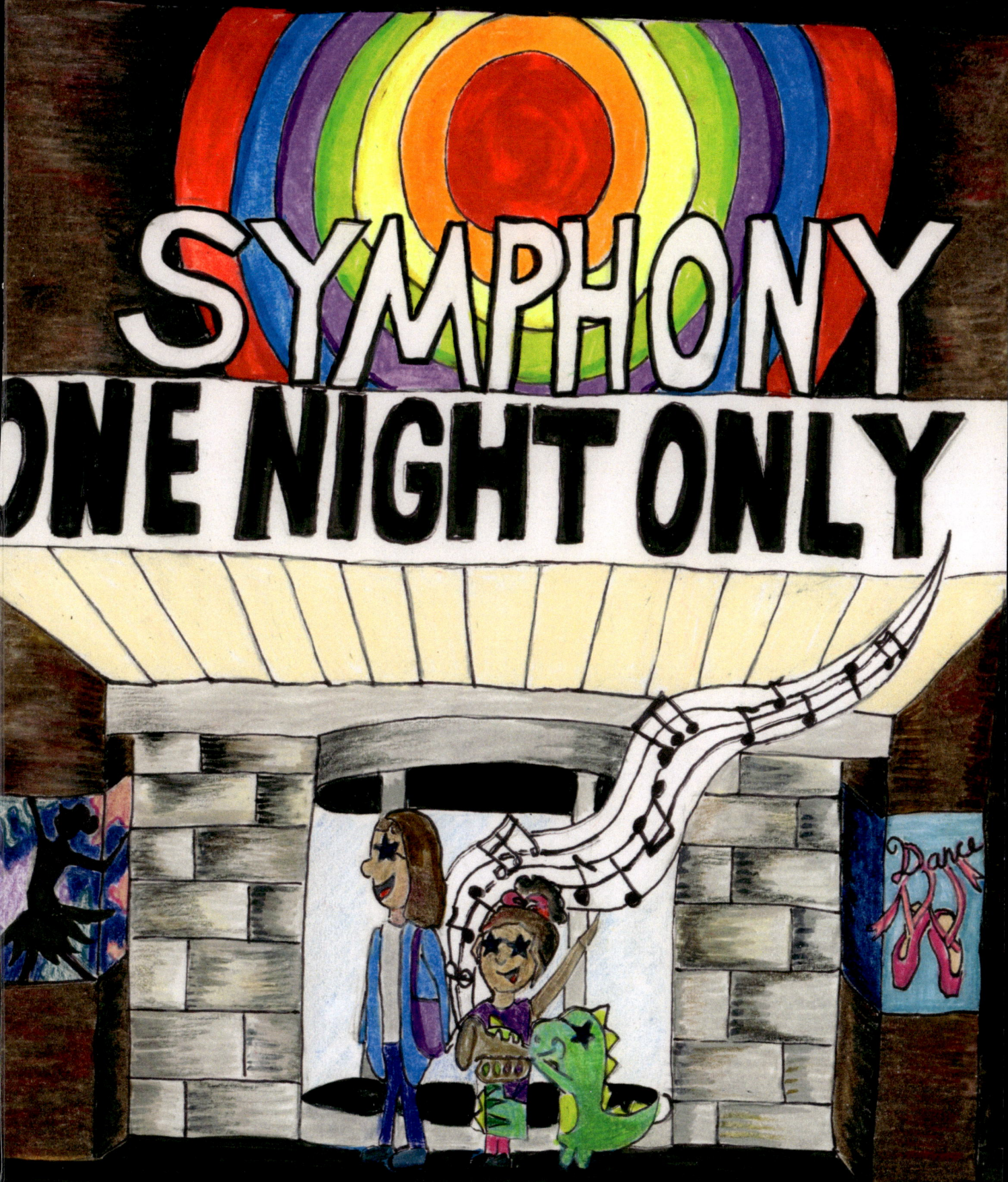

"The music makes my heart dance," Alex shared as she leaped and left the concert hall with her Mama, hand in hand.

What Makes SymFUNNY so Funny?

It's all about **HOMONYMS.** What are homonyms?
Homonyms are words that sound the same but have different meanings.

Base
in the game of baseball or softball, one of the four stations that must be reached in turn to score a run

Bass
a member of a family of instruments that is the lowest in pitch

Chords
a group of (typically three or more) notes sounded together

OR

Cords
thin, flexible string or rope made from several twisted strands

Conductor
a person in charge of a train, streetcar, or other transportation, who collects fares and sells tickets

OR

a person who directs the performance of an orchestra, choir or musical ensemble

Horns
a hard permanent outgrowth, often curved and pointed, found in pairs on the heads of cattle, sheep, goats, giraffes, etc.

OR

a sound-making device used as a warning on a car, bike or other vehicle

OR

a wind instrument, conical in shape or wound into a spiral, originally made from an animal horn (now typically brass) and played by lip vibration

Notes
a short informal letter or written message

OR

a single tone of definite pitch made by a musical instrument or the human voice

Scales
a device having a series of marks at regular intervals in a line used in measuring something

OR

an arrangement of the notes in any system of music in ascending or descending order of pitch

Strings
a piece of string used to tie around or attach to something

OR

the stringed instruments in an orchestra

Symfunny
a silly book designed to take children on an introductory symphonic musical adventure

Symphony
(especially in names of orchestras) short for symphony orchestra

OR

an elaborate musical composition for full orchestra, typically in four movements

Definitions from Oxford Languages (with the exception of Symfunny)